Essence of Love

Copyright © 2008 by Matthew Lohr

All rights reserved

Table of contents

Dream speak	1
Essence of Love	5
Exotic Glances	9
Her Smile	13
I Wish	17
Love from the Heavens	21
Life to Love	25
Meant for Me	29
Your Nature	33
The Song She Sings	37
The Vows	41
Thoughts of Her	45
Slow Burn	49
Warrior's Daughter	53
Nosferatu	57
Midnight Melodies	61
Love Chamber	65
Come Together	69
Missing You	73
One Note	77
Its funny	81
God Dictation	85
One Look	89
Amaretto	93
Intimate Ways	97

Dream Speak

I've seen her
In sequences of dream schemes
Made for dream fiends
In which fiends dream
Of love scenes
That are so serene
They are any thing
But routine
And she stood in the center
Like she does in my universe
And her smile
Looks on me like sun burst
And her sun rays
Bring warmth on cold days
Brings new comfort to my life
To make me let go of old ways

I want to make sure
Lady no longer has to sing the blues
On her dark days
I want to be the one to bring her new hues
Take the gray away from her skies
So she can see skies blue as ocean depths
And be the one
To make her catch her breath
Put just a little
More life in her step
And take away
All the tears in life she wept
And when she sleeps
I want to live in her dream space
Eternally
Because I know that dreams take
Moments and last
Lifetimes in blinks of an eye
And as long as we dream
I know that I can lie
With her in my arms
Until the time, time ends
And these dreams perfectly
Let my mind send

Dream notes
Filled with beautiful rose fields
And nurturing these dreams
Could only mean these dream yield
Young dreams
And I love her fun dreams
And I know that we
Really only just have one dream
To share together
And we can have dream weather
On our dream day
Know our dreams will never
End because we can bend
Reality live in dream time
Look past our troubles
And grow dreams in the mean time
Reclaim lost dreams
And make them come alive again
Or make new one
So we can break those old trends
And live together
In our very own dream space
With gourmet dreams
And we can make these dreams taste

However we choose
Because our destiny is a dream state
Yet it seems
No matter how hard I dream fate
Is something I can't escape
So I pray one day I just die in these dreams
Because she
Only seems to live in my dreams

Essence of Love

As beautiful as that of
The Garden of Eden's is the scent you leave
And I just want to live
The rest of my life with your scent to breathe
And I see myself with thee
Because you make me a better me
Than without you
I could ever begin to hope to be
And if eyes are truly
The windows to the soul
Then your eyes must be mine
Because in you I see myself whole
So for you
I would walk through hellfire
And look for new ways
To love you until my life expires

See I want to be
The one to bring light to your dark days
And bring comfort and warmth
To the place where your heart stays
Lay with you where angels do
On clouds in the skies above
Because my heart lies above
Troubled waters in your love
And we can live
In the place were love lives
Because to you I have
And endless supply of love to give
Because you replenish me
When my insides run dry
And wipe away my tears
Before I even begin to cry
And I want to try to love you
More than love itself can love
Simply for the fact
You give my heart the gentlest rubs
And kisses
Making me long for memories of tomorrow
And have me looking
Through history for a way to borrow

From lovers of past
So I can secure the future with you
Because the only thing I want to do
Is live my life with you
So through times of trouble
We can rise like bubbles
And if it seems I am slipping
Then my efforts I'll redouble
I'll have angels sing you
To sleep with heavenly lullabies
And have doves sing to you
When then sun rises in morning skies
Have the trees
Shield you from the cold breeze
And on holy days
You can find me on my knees
Praying for this love
To be as vast as the universe
And we can sit on new planets
Just like the first two on this earth
I will be your Adam
And I want you for my eve
Our love will be a new genesis
For all of our descendants to believe

Our loves tales
Are just proof of creation
Because when we make love
We spawn new civilizations
And the sensations you give
Breathe life into me
And as my starts to beat in sync with yours
We begin to be
One
Set of planets that revolve
Around each other
And we evolve
Beyond physical
To the heavens above
Felt by all because you
Are the essence of love

Exotic Glances

Exotic glances

Give way to thoughts of chances

Of romantic dances

The captivating smile only enhances

Fantasies of future days

Spent with you on ocean shores

Wondering what

Fate just may hold in store

I see you

Looking at me looking your way

And I'm wondering

If today is the day destiny comes my way

You make my heart say

Things may be better left unsaid

But if I don't speak

This may be the day that I dread

And I may look back
On this day as missed love
The day I let pass
An angel straight from heaven above
See I have future thoughts
Of us sharing special times
Playing love songs
On your heart stings written about past times
See I wonder if
You are wondering if I
May speak
Or should I just keep passing by
Leaving you
As the perfect rose untouched
Because the look in your eyes
Maybe just a little too much
Too beautiful for me
To look upon every day
But I see you with me
Loving in every way
Love is made to be
So we can make melodies
Let our hearts be unleashed
Because you seem to settle me

So we can run

From here to the edge of forever

Let heart flames burn brighter

Than the sun so they never

Fade away

And I will never stay away

For longer than a heart beat

And we can just sail away

On endless seas

Letting love be our guide

Ride high

And move along with ocean tides

Sails powered by nothing

But the wind songs

Live in love's house

But never stay in long

Because your heart

Is the only place I want to stay inside

So we'll run off in sunsets

And there we can hide

In fairytales

Where jack's beanstalk will never be as high

As my love for you

And just for fun we can fly

Away with peter pan
To never land with Tinkerbelle
You can be my Cinderella
I'll be your prince charming and we can tell
Our tales
To each one of the seven dwarfs
Skip the witches of the west
And east as we head north
To build our own dreams
And ice cream castles
Writing everlasting tales
So we can live without the hassles
Of endings
Just spend time lending
Nourishment to nature
Because your glance is sending
Me to heights
I never even knew existed
And maybe
It invited me in and I missed it
So I'll just take my stance
Next to you take my chances
To say hello and with you
I want to share never ending glances

Her Smile

Her smile set my heart ablaze
So to her I spoke in smoke signals
Rewrote quotes from angels
And sent them as notes by seagulls
Who traveled paths along ancient shores
Coastal beaches on islands in the tropics
Though most days she is far away
I keep her near right here in my hearts pocket
You see she may not always
Be with me physically
So interwoven intricacies
Universally keep her connected to me
Our lives have blended
My hearts scars have mended
And it seems
That time and space have bended

To place us in the same space
With time to waste
And the cleansing rain
That has life's pain erased
Because with her
I want to create new yesterdays
Reminisce about new yesteryears
While we bask in tropical sunrays
And when she isn't here
I still have roses in the winter time
Because my heart and mind
Is still lost in a time
When we were holding hand
Under waterfalls
And I have no fear
Because she is always here when my heart calls
And I watch the sun fall
And the stars rise until sunrise
Every time I look
Into the most beautiful eyes my eyes
Have ever seen
She is god's angel sent to me
And I am blessed
Because she was meant for me

And I for her
So my heart is her open door
And I pick daisies saying
She loves me she loves me more
Than I have ever
Been loved before
And when I feel I told her enough
I tell her some more
That she
Drives my heart wild
She didn't have to say hello
She had me at her smile
The way it curves
Like crescent moons
Makes my heart smile
And fills up the empty room
In my soul
And her love has taken hold
And her beauty
Is too much for mere mortals to hold
And she calms my world
And brings out my inner child
And the only thing she has to do
Is smile

I Wish

I wish
Every morning I could hear the birds sing
And every day
I would hear wedding bells ring
And I could always see the sun rise
And at mid day
It would begin again
So it would always be a new day
And it would set
On nights with no regret
Leaving me
With memories I never want to forget
I wish I
Could fly so high
And live
Amongst the birds in the sky

Vacation deep

Amongst the ocean depths

Always see new sights

That take away my breath

Hear the angel's sing

About the glories to come

So the whole world

Can come together as one

I wish I could walk through

Through the Garden of Eden

Smell new scents

With every breath that I breathe in

I wish I could

Wade in the water with doves on my shoulder

Bring warmth

So nights no longer get any colder

Sit on African plains

Watch the gazelles as they run

I wish that I

Could become one with the rays of the sun

Or the rays

That I feel when you smile on me

That are so intense

That at times

I feel one with thee

And I need no doves
With your head on my shoulder
And your love
Brings the warmth so nights are no colder
And gazelles
Are not nearly as graceful as you
The Garden of Eden
Is not half as beautiful as you
The sunset and sunrise
Do not compare to your eyes
And when I'm lost in you
Day break may never come and I wouldn't even realize
Birds can't even sing your song
And don't get along like you and I
And our love is so deep
The ocean's bottom seems too high
And skies look so low
Next to the height's you take me
And if I only heard
Church bells once for us you would make me
 The happiest man
To dare stand before god's eyes
Asking him to bless
The two of us in our lives

So if I had only one I wish

It would be to spend all my days with you

Because when I'm with you

All my wishes always come true

Love from the Heavens

I want to see you at days end
And when days begin I want to grin because it's your face I see
And if we lived in broken down shacks
I wouldn't care because with you is the place for me
And if the land was barren
And you were the only sight to see
I want you to know that life
Would still be alright for me
And I want to be your man
And I need you for my wife
So if we died in each others arms
We could be reborn in the afterlife
And after night falls
I know you are my sunrise
So it can be dark for all time
Because you know in my eyes

I have your light

Which makes my harvest grow

And off of rivers in valley's low

I see your inner sun glow

Making our life

Just like island paradise

And the steadiness of your loves

Assures I never have to think twice

About what the world holds

Because you are my gold and diamonds

Found at ends of leprechauns rainbows

And bring me peace in any situation I'm in

So hold my hand

As we run on beaches with pink sand

And let me

Kneel before the place in which you stand

Speak to you

As Romeo did to Juliet

Leave our mark

So our descendants never forget

Love we made days we stayed

In the midst of each others arms

And the way I shielded

You from worlds of harm

And they worship
The pedestal on which I place you
So they can look
In the same direction which I faced you
And reread my words
As if they were holy text
And let them
Understand these times so in the correct context
They can feel it
As you and I feel so uplifted
And in case
Any in the universe has missed it
We can travel to pyramids
Rewrite each and every hieroglyphic
Leave words cryptic
So only the most gifted of mystics
Can decrypt it
Re tell story in its pure form
So people feel safe
In the eye of the most pure storm
As much as I
Have felt safe in the arms of your love
Knowing that this love
Can only come from the heavens above

Life to Love

You can give life
The love it needs
And give love
Its very life
And my life
On most days
Used to cut me Just like a knife
But now it's
Slow massages at days end
And although I know
These days may end
In the morn
They always begin again
Because your love
Just has no end

And most times I'm
Just lost up in it
So my skies
Always have no limits
So even if days ruin me
I know you still love me
So I fight my battles
With strength from heaven above see
So I will
Always continue to win
And when battles bring me down
You turn my frowns to grins
So in your arms
I simply win again
And you give me
The strength to begin again
And the wisdom to know
I can win by letting battles go
So I can sit with you
By the river of love and watch the water flow
To us
And the love flows through us
And destiny makes me see
That nature always knew us

As a couple
Even before the days of the sun
And it seems that in love
We were raised as one
You gave love to my life
And in your love I found life
So I need to know
Will you be my wife?
Because I can't live
Another day without you
And my poetry will
Always be about you
It's like I can't even see
Without you
Because you bring light
Like an angel so I could never doubt you
So I want you to see
Me down on bended knee
Finally learning to let
My heart speak free
Do you hear it?
As it speaks to thee
Saying at the altar

I want you to meet with me
Saying I do
Because I do too
Love you
More than I think even angels do
And I want to give your life love
And give life to this love
So we can always shine
Just like the stars above

Meant for Me

I remember
Our last kiss as if it was
Just a second ago
My lips still quiver because it was
The only kiss
That truly shook my heart
Left its inscription
So I want to try and start
That kiss over
From it's beginning
You see it left
My soul still grinning
From right to left
And since you left
I am still
Holding the same breath

My eyes still closed

Because I don't want to see

That you

Are no longer here in front of me

And I still feel

Your aura here as if you never went

And I feel blessed

Because I know god lent

His perfect angel

Only to me

And he may

Want me to share what I was blessed to see

But I find

It a little hard to describe you

Because there are no words

To tell what I found inside you

Or to relate

The feeling you made in me

So others must learn

To see the man I will begin to be

Lest I create new adjectives

Adverbs for new verbs

Or speak in tongues

That only prophets have heard

In meditation
Because the sensations
I still feel
Are encrypted in revelations
Prophesied about
In the book of genesis
So I foresee
There will be no end to this
So I wait
Until god returns us together
And if I must
Then I shall wait until forever
Because if that
Is what is meant to be
Then it must be
Because I know you were meant for me

Your Nature

Natural settings
Made from natural beginnings
Made for natural weddings
Might prevent unnatural endings
So naturally I
Want to make new beginnings with you
And we can do
The things nature intended us to do
Like walk through fields
Or sit on rocks on the hilltops
And just look over the plains
Because sights of you still stop
My heart beat
Because you are a wonder of nature
And I think trees
Sway in the breeze just to imitate the

Natural way
In which your hips sway
And doves circle above
Because they want to know which way
You go
And your love flows like the rivers
And like night fall
Sends chills down my spine making me shiver
And warms me up
Like morning sunrays and some days
I get so high on you
I feel like taking off like birds with no runways
We can let our roots grow
Intertwine in the underground
Love like the evergreens
So our love is never summer bound
Live like the bluebirds
And never sing any blue songs
Just make soothing melodies
Like the new streams I'll love you long
Like summer days
In winter time I long to keep you warm
Like the sun
And in spring we'll be reborn

Like the flowers bloom
And the lush green of the new grass
And grow together again
Just like we did in years past
We can share tears
Like those from the rain clouds
At expectations of new life
So nature is the same its future remains now
In your hand
Growing in your womb
And soon we'll
Be watching a new flower bloom
So we can have a new us
With new ways
And as one being
Look forward to new days
Se we came from nature
So we can return to nature
And in the meantime
I just want a taste of your nature
The juices of your fruits
Live in the loins of love with you
Ride in the skies
On the clouds above with you

And I know ashes

To ashes and dust unto dust

But before I return

To this earth if I must

I want to my

Nature to mix with yours

Because I know that you

Must be the elixir for

All the ills

I had in my past seasons

And that my tree has new branches

You're the reason

And so that I

May be able to better relate to

The world around me

I just want to live in your nature

The Song She Sings

Her voice
Can calm seas in hurricanes
Or break the silence of night
And shatter window panes
Her melody
Brought peace to my spirit
And her tune is such
That none other comes near it
And she
Was killing me softly
With her song
And I didn't care if it cost me
My soul
Because with out her song
It could never be whole

So I just drift along
To the tempo she sets
And her rhythm
Makes my life
Worth living
And I can only sleep
After hearing her night song
And waking in the morn
Without her song is so wrong
She said her eyes
Are only beautiful when they look at me
And her world
First shook with me
So when she first
Sang in my ear the words get here
I knew I
Would always need her near
To my personal atmosphere
To my skies clear
And the first time she walked away
I felt one tear
That dried when she looked back
Blew that one kiss to me
Whispered that she
Already misses me

And I loved that
Because I already wrote that
And destiny makes me believe she
Is the reason I spoke that
So I already know what's on
The horizon so as the sun's rising
I'm thinking of the way
That her I'll be surprising
With a poetic question
And just one ring
Because I want to hear
The way she sings
Yes to me
Bless me again in my ear
You see she
Already said to get here
So I am here and she's here
We have love here
We live on the clouds
So no one is above here
Or her because she
Is the wind beneath my wings
And her wings of love
Are as beautiful as the song she sings

The Vows

Its funny how
Crowded rooms can feel like empty places
And total strangers
Can be just like familiar faces
Because in a crowded room
I see no others
And the first time I saw you
You seemed like an old lover
Drawing me past
Scenes that were all too familiar
And leaving me
Without an ounce of the will to
Resist Or see
What should have been plain to me
That with you
Is the only place I would remain to be

So now I know
I could never be too close to you
And of myself
I could never give most to you
Because you
Already have all of me
And what ever I have
I will give all to thee
My existence
Has found its purpose within you
Because before you
I was lost on what to do
I was a warrior
With no battles to fight
Like days
That existed without the sunlight
Like oceans
That had no waves to break
Like birds and bees
With no love to make
I used to write books
That had no words
Now I have words
That run out of ears in which to be heard

It's so absurd

That before you I don't remember breathing

Now I'm thankful

For every breath I feel leaving

My lungs

Because they leave room for rose scents

And my eyes

Are blessed with sights heaven scent

My ears

Are always filled with angel songs

And nights with you

Have replaced days that were too long

And I

Want to walk the path of god with you

And be your shelter

From days that seem too hard for you

I want to be your everything

Because you are all things to me

I want to bring you

All the joy you bring to me

See you are the beginning

To my life the end to my troubles

The force that turns

Relics of my past into rubble

The ocean

That can change my whole coast line

The two of us

Can raise our glasses and toast lines

Of Solomon's song

Because now we live them

So in turn

The two of us as one can give them

New meaning

Because you mean the world to me

And I know

You have always been the only girl for me

So I devote

My entire soul to you

And I want to be

The only one holding you

Because like Picasso with no paint

I without you have no worth

And that thought alone

Makes the thoughts in my mind hurt

So on this day

I pledge the rest of my days

To be the one loving you

From now until the end of always

Thoughts of Her

We wrote poetry with
No pen's ink or pencil's lead
Threw away all paper
There were no words to be said
Tossed out all etiquette
And I'm not one for fashion
And neighbors heard only
Poetic sounds of passion
Like heart beats
That beat together like
Doves singing in harmony
At morning's first light
And I'm blessed
Just to have stood next to her
And her karma is too pure
To even think about sex with her

So I made love to her soul
Like she already did mine
And as we laid
With spirits intertwined
I began to find
I was reading god's perfect poetic lines
In her curves
And her fruits nectar
Keeps my third eye blurred
My inner voice slurred
Because I'm intoxicated
With thoughts of her
And these thoughts
Are of long term
And yearn for her is strong
My heart burns
My head turns
To see if she
Is still next to me
But no so these
Thoughts become complex to me
Yet her footsteps
I still hear so she walks with me
And in moments of clarity
I hear her still talk to me

So in dreams I speak back
And I know it's a fact that
We live in dream space
So I can just relax that
Thought of her
Never being able to be here
Because I imagine I
Make the melody that she hear
In her ear when she dreams
In day time and in night time
I want to be the warmth
She feels run in her spine
And those thoughts
Make days filled with rain
Turn to sunshine
Ease heart strains remove love pains
And visions of her eyes
Can replace the sunrise in spring time
Create music in my life
Because she is the perfect baseline
My last lifeline
And my lifetime
Isn't complete
Till I make her smile shine

And bloom like a rose
Her lips like the pedals
Because the shield on my heart
She melts all the metal
Leaving my heart bare
And easy to be caught
Then keeps it in hers
Easing all my thoughts

Slow Burn

She's my slow burn

Small fire that keeps my soul warm

Strong woman turn

Shelter keep me dry through the whole storm

I need her

By my side to bandage wounds

Inflicted by demons

Trying to seal the doors on my tomb

Because she

Will forever be my eternity

Herbal remedies

And for her needs she turns to me

And I fulfill them

Till her cup runneth over

I skip past rose fields
And look for her amongst the clover
Each one four leaf
Because with luck I find her there
And nature is refreshed
From the scents of her hair
She's my everything
My everywhere the sole reason
My soul's reasons
To stand for her in all seasons
I'm breathing
Just to fill my lungs with her essence
So I can hold onto her
When she wanders from my presence
When I look for her
The North Star leads me in her direction
Constellation form in her form
Confirming our cosmic connections
Intersecting in
Universes where angels rehearse
Enchanting melodies
With the most romantic of verses
With bursts of
Trumpet notes mixed with harp strings
And children dance
And sing with the joy the heart brings

When one loves

As I do her as she loves in return

Because she

Keeps me warm with that slow burn

And her fire

I protect till my life runs out

You see when it comes to her

My life is nothing without

Warrior's Daughter

She
Is the daughter of Shaka
So I have a lot to prove
Because the king's daughter
Is who I want for my queen so I move
Not like crook do but
More like a man and take a stand
Because the god of warriors
Wants to know my plans
So I fight not the enemy
But for the love of my people
To show I am my people
Yet my people have no equal
So first to battle
In hunt I bring first kill
Push past former limits
Test boundaries that test skills

I am

First to heed king's call

Because he has treasure

And of it I want all

And he knows my desires

And keeps the prize

Far from my eyes

So I prove that I a wise

And wait

Patient let her know I am worthy

Enough

For my people to serve me

As they serve

Her father my king the god

Of warriors

Of all earth on which lions trod

The trees on which

Birds sing monkeys swing

And over the oceans

Which eternally bring

Sustenance

To generations yet to come

Across which

We can travel as one

Until kingdom comes

Unto us in our own land

In a kingdom which

We fashion with our own hand
So I stand
Spear ready so the Serengeti
Respect my
Status as warrior mind steady
Waiting for the day
The god of warriors King Shaka
Deems I am worthy
To hold the hand of his daughter

Nosferatu

I was hungry for
A new sense of intimacy
That seemed could only
Be fulfilled by her and she
Was always hungry for
A little bit more
That what current times
Held in store
And years without feeding
Left my heart needing
Nourishment beyond
Stages of fresh seeding
And she needed mature love
Beyond occasional rubs
Eyes only meeting halfway
And uninspired I love

You's

She needed consistence
And I consistently needed
To close up this distance
Between love
And lonely winter nights
That never ended
With no one holding tight
And no morning sun
To wake up to
No one to make mistakes with
And no one to make up to
And this hunger
Turned into addiction
Not wanting a cure
Just looking for the right fix and
Hunger needs feeding
So we fed together
Off of each other
Knowing this hunger would never
Subside
And not feeding is suicide
And this hunger I used to fear
I can no longer hide

And she controls mine
As I do hers
Intravenously
Instantaneously we feed
Each others
Needs completely we heed
Calls from the souls
Of ancient lovers screaming
Because this is love which others fear
And of which their dreaming
Love mature nourishing
Love so cleansing and pure
A love so addicting
That it always leaves me hungry for her

Midnight Melodies

I want to play
Melodies at midnight
Because I'm tired
Of days from which clouds hid light
That turned into nights
That held no starlight
No first star to see
And I need to see star bright
I'm tired of noons
That hold no tunes
Just empty choruses
Hear in dark corners of my room
I want to string
Midnight melodies together
So that forever
Holds our baselines together

So harmonize with me
Till these harmonies make misty
Moments in history
From days which you missed me
Because I missed you
And I've been through
Too many sad songs
Along rocky roads so now into
You
Is where I want to be
And treble clefs
Tell how I'm wanting thee
With notes
Written at the stroke of
Midnight so melodies
Play in the hope of
Love
With quartets of angels that harmonize
And at sunrise
The sun will realize
That it can't outshine us
And birds singing in perfect key
Could never match
Our midnight melody

So our love time

May span octave ranges

Greater than

Pavarotti so we'll have ages

To write compositions

Greater than that of Mozart

And Beethoven

And I truly know of no art

By Da' Vinci could convince me

You aren't god's masterpiece

So let's spend time

So we can master these

Choreographies

Of harmonies and we

Can collaborate

On love notes and write these

Bars in stone

As hieroglyphics in pyramids

Singing nursery rhymes

Just like when we were kids

Keeping time

Better than metronomes

Living in base tones

Just like they were home

Playing piano keys

Patiently waiting

For midnight to come

While anticipating

The lullabies

I love you telling me

So meet me at twelve

So we

Can make midnight melodies

Love Chamber

She entered

The center of my love chamber

Broke down my

Heart cells with no remainder

And it was plain to

See she was to remain here

Bring life joy

And erase the pain here

So she renewed my

Life supply and I

Felt her flow

Through me feeding my

Soul what it needs

And she just wanted to stay here

Inside of mon couer

Like a child and just play here

On love swings
Keeping time like pendulums
Love notes pending
Rose blooms then sending them
In dozens daily
On bended knee I say thee
Prayers for her ears
So I may make the
Chambers of my heart
Into palace chambers worthy
Of her because I
Have one purpose to serve the
Kingdom that serves her
With heavenly treasures
For her pleasure
As I have only to be measured
By the queen
Who chooses to stand with me
And if her eyes tear
I may move swiftly
To dry drops
Before her cheeks wet
Because days spent apart
Make weeks get

Lonely

So I long for her to hold me

On winter nights

That are ever so cold she

Keeps me warm

By using my old pains to

Keep the fires burning

Here in my love's chamber

Come Together

Let's come together
Find heaven together
Flood the dry plains
With oceans change the weather
We'll rain together
In the middle of clear skies
See the stars at noon
Looking with clear eyes
As I follow scents
Leading to a warm space
For a taste
Of forbidden fruit from your place
In which is hidden
The nectar of your essence
Leaving me intoxicated
Sedated in your presence

Because you move me
So move with me
And we can make
The earth move so swiftly
Into this tightly
And out of this world
And back in
And around till stars swirl
And waterfalls
Start to flow endlessly
Because the only end
Is when we
Arrive there together
And stay there forever
Holding one another
Promising to never
Stay away long
Here's where we belong
And the sounds of our passion
Make the most erotic song
Bringing us back to the place
Where we first started
Smiles on our faces
Like we never parted

Yet we move mountains

Not caring where times goes

Because I'm just trying

To go and make ocean's flow

Over again and I

Just want to fill you

From the inside

Out so lady will you

Come with me

Until the edge of forever

And there we

Can find heaven together

Missing You

I have these passing
Thoughts of glancing
Over moon lit waters
Watching them dancing
Over ocean shores
On nights with cool breeze
Hearing the wind
As it blows through trees
Makings sounds
That remind me
Of the way
You would come behind me
Arms wrapped around me
Warm kisses placed so right
That always seemed
To lead to warm nights

Nights that made me
Cherish mornings spent with you
Leading forward toward
Days meant to be spent with you
With sun glistening
Over the same waters with waves
Still dancing on the same shores
With the two of us misbehaving
Passing thoughts
Of nights filled with starry skies
Being lost in love
Looking in star filled eyes
That belonged to you
Leaving me longing to be with you
Longing for this love
To flourish on open seas with you
I have thoughts
That are ever so passing
Like these waves
That just seem to keep on passing
Back to open seas
Wondering if we can reopen these
Lines of communication
Thoughts begging please

Thoughts placed
Like messages in bottles
Thrown to the waters
Hoping for answers to fill hollow
Nights
That are lonely with thoughts
Like these waves
That just seem to be caught
Passing
Back out to sea
I'm hoping these thoughts
Aren't just stuck
Here with me
I'm hoping these thoughts
Are out there with you
And not just passing
Because I'm here missing you

One Note

I could hear
The rhythms of her body sing the blues to me
In melodies that melded with my soul
Like they were use to me
Her treble intertwined
With my baseline
As I read the notes
She had written in her waist line
I knew it would take time
To finish this masterpiece
And knew I had to
Write this in line with my master's piece
Of poetic design
He left in scriptures
Because I knew others wouldn't hear
So these words are written as pictures

Hieroglyphics
For future mystics to deliver
As life lessons
Taught to students through slivers
Of music
Rewritten and reused in symphonies
Played on street corners
Giving young lovers epiphanies
Used in nursery rhymes
Sung as lullabies
At midnight
Just as she gets all of my
Love
Because there is no other
Sheet of music
I place above her
And together
We are instruments angels play
Creating heavenly sounds played
In intimate lounges where angles stay
Notes written
As if together they were made to be
Harmonies created
From winter nights she laid with me

Until dew settles

On flowers in spring blooms

From mountain tops

To bells that ring in rooms

Where young lovers

Sing their nuptials

Over underlying tones

That are ever so subtle

They are reminiscent

Of wind songs filled with angel quotes

And in the key of my life

She is my one note

It's Funny

It's funny
I find myself thinking
Feeling like
As if I was drinking
Mind blinking
In the middle of afternoons
Wondering if
Days will finish faster and soon
I can dream again
Because that's were she lives
So I live to sleep
Because in dreams she gives
Love just like
Angels intend for it to be
And her heart
She always gives it to me

So I pray
That morning may never come
And in dreams
That we can forever run
Away from
The place from which the sun comes
And I can live with the feeling
That one feels when one comes
To the realization
This is the place where destiny
Meets revelations
So I am ready to give the rest of me
The best of me
Till there is none left of me
And she
Takes the last breath of me
And we
Can live where dreams take eternity
Because her love does
And will forever burn in me
Because I
Am her Moses and she speaks to me
Like burning bushes and makes
Me weak in knees

So I kneel before her
And pray for more of her
And offer all of
What I have in store for her
And beg
That she accepts my offering
Because I tithe
Until plates containing my offering
For her
Are filled beyond capacity
And hope she
Understands my audacity
To dream
And if not I don't really care
Because when I wake
She is no longer there

God's Dictation

This is
Dictation I wrote from on high
And I
Now admit the fact that I
Never wrote
Quotes spoke in my own words
Just hoped
Words I spoke is what she heard
Because my words
Were never worthy of her
So I pray
For words to serve me so her
Spirit will
Hear it when I speak these
Nouns and
Verbs with adjectives as I seek these

Spiritual phrases
To fill pages with paragraphs
That may
Speak to half her beauty as I ask
God to bless
Me with the courage to speak
Meek words
Week to week so now I seek
To sit on peaks
Of elevated consciousness
Concentrating
Waiting for her to catch on to this
Message I
Try to send to her soul
Looking to mend
Old wounds wanting a whole
Love to share
Without cares of heart pains
Looking to share
Love to erase these hearts stains
Left by
Loves that only took love
Making me
Love to just look above

For love
That maybe willing to love back
Live with me
On sandy beaches in loves shack
Not caring
That love is our only shelter
To protect us
When rain and hail pelt the
Roof of our
Palm covered house of bamboo
House she is
Willing to commit to and I am to
So I sit through
Deliverance of words
Spoken to me in chorus and verse
That I write
In midst of lonely nights
By fire so bright
Wrapped in melodies so tight
That my sight
Is open to the revelations
So I can continue
To write to her
All of god's dictation

One Look

One look
And her eyes took
Me years past seduction
As my lips longed
For introduction I begged for interruption
To a mundane life
Hoping to erase strained life
Mentally drinking her
Thinking she would be the same wife
My dreams hold
Yet my dreams told
Me too many lies
And I'm now too wise to let my dreams fold
Into reality
Which is no longer real to me
And I'm tired
From letting these women heal through me

Yet she took me
Past there to places past where
Memories held pains
Left in place from loves that were last there
With words unheard
Spoken through batted eyelash
And quick winks
Making me think that I last
Forever in her eyes
As she has been in mine
Hoping the two of us
Can last hours past time
Through time to times
When time no longer matters
To we have love
That is stronger than that of
Atlas and Hercules
And make captains of the seas
Fear our love storms
Created from the way that we breathe
For one another
She's my confidant my lover
Through her
Burning love I've discovered

Yet not on step

Has she even took with me

See I'm left exhausted

And all she ever did was just look at me

Amaretto

When we kiss

Your lips taste like amaretto

And when I'm holding you

I find it's kind of hard to let go

Because your eyes

Have me hypnotized

So mesmerized

That when I look in them I feel like I see the sunrise

And the sunset

And this moment

I'll never forget

So this moment

I might live to regret

Because this moment

Could never be forever

And the two of us well

We might not last together

See were both grown
And can weather the storm
You
Might seek other places to get warm
So walk with me come
Talk with me and let me whisper
I want you to be my miss
And let me be your mister
Your king
I'll build empires for you
And when armies come
I will breathe fire for you
I'll build temples
And name entire gardens after you
We can take fairytale journeys
So I can find unicorns to capture for you
And air is not worth breathing
Unless it's filled with your scent
And if this love is not enough
These words I'll reinvent
I'll speak in tongues
That were reserved for the gods
And travel paths to you
On which only ancient prophets have trod

I want to share with you

Lay with my soul bare with you

Get high on this love

And fly through the air with you

Because I think we

Can have it all together

And I want the two of us

To rise and fall together

Catch each other

And never let go

But if you must

Can I have one more kiss because I already miss the taste of your amaretto

Intimate Ways

She

Touched my soul in intimate ways

And began to raise me from the grave past loves laid me in

And it was jus in the nick of time because the sunshine started to fade as the walls long since began caving in

And she remade me in

Images of her heart while chipping away the concrete mine was incased in

Made me smile as I used to as a child

And all the while she was steadily replacing

Memories of bad times

That hurt more than reworked reoccurring thoughts of those sad times

Each one replaced with those

Fantasies of fun we haven't even yet had times

And when we kissed I felt her heart beat
In sync with mine through her lips which
Reminded me of all those
Romantic days which I had missed
Yet like the raven
I shall miss never more
Because I want to stay inside her love doors
And I promise to love her more
Than Romeo and Cyrano
Than Samson ever loved Delilah
And if times get trying and we find love dying
Then I will simply try to
Give her my next rib so it can live
Through a new Genesis past Revelations
To be witnessed by future generations
Only to be told
Through poetic narrations
With no words
Over the melodies of heart songs
Longing to be written
Scripted up upon
Church walls ancient halls longing to be discovered
Uncovered by archaeologists
Harbored by love sects that write love texts
That are used by psychologists

To heal pains
Felt by Cleopatra and Marc Anthony
Make armies lay down their swords
Have warlords sign peace accords and calm the angry seas
Because her love
Is so pure
It feeds the fountain of youth
And no matter what lies the devil may say
Her love is the truth
Proof
That my soul existed since the beginning days
Now just as it once was
When she first touched it in intimate ways

Acknowledgments

I would like to give thanks to those that have inspired me, encouraged me and gave me an outlet to express my thoughts and feelings.

To the crew at Warm Wednesdays (Five Seasons), Jacqui Cummings, proprietor of Notre Maison, The crew at The Art of Conversation and at Interpretation Sundays for providing a great atmosphere for live poetry.

To the crew at The Ground Floor for always providing an intimate atmosphere for writing and their non stop promotion of my art.

To my friends Marvin, Marcus, Marilyn and Ricky for always being there.

To my parents for proving that true love does exist.

To Chantele who is a constant reminder that impossible is just a word to be forgotten.

To God.

And remember to Live well, Laugh often and Love as much as possible.

www.ingramcontent.com/pod-product-compliance
Lightning Source LLC
Chambersburg PA
CBHW060357050426
42449CB00009B/1776